A Woman's War Record, 1861-1865

Mrs. Septima Maria Levy Collis, Septima Maria Collis

Nabu Public Domain Reprints:

You are holding a reproduction of an original work published before 1923 that is in the public domain in the United States of America, and possibly other countries. You may freely copy and distribute this work as no entity (individual or corporate) has a copyright on the body of the work. This book may contain prior copyright references, and library stamps (as most of these works were scanned from library copies). These have been scanned and retained as part of the historical artifact.

This book may have occasional imperfections such as missing or blurred pages, poor pictures, errant marks, etc. that were either part of the original artifact, or were introduced by the scanning process. We believe this work is culturally important, and despite the imperfections, have elected to bring it back into print as part of our continuing commitment to the preservation of printed works worldwide. We appreciate your understanding of the imperfections in the preservation process, and hope you enjoy this valuable book.

Septima M. Collis.

A

WOMAN'S WAR RECORD

1861–1865

BY

SEPTIMA M. COLLIS

(MRS. GEN'L. CHARLES H. T. COLLIS)

NEW YORK AND LONDON

G. P. PUTNAM'S SONS

The Knickerbocker Press

1889

A
WOMAN'S WAR RECORD

1861–1865

BY

SEPTIMA M. COLLIS

(MRS. GENL. CHARLES H. T. COLLIS)

NEW YORK AND LONDON
G. P. PUTNAM'S SONS
The Knickerbocker Press
1889

COPYRIGHT BY
SEPTIMA M. COLLIS
1889

The Knickerbocker Press
Electrotyped and Printed by
G. P. Putnam's Sons

DEDICATION.

TO HER WHOSE TEACHINGS AND EXAMPLE MOULDED MY
CHILDHOOD, WHOSE BLESSINGS AND WHOSE PRAYERS
FOLLOWED AND SUSTAINED ME IN MATURE LIFE,
AND WHOM GOD I HOPE WILL SPARE FOR
MANY AND MANY A YEAR THAT I MAY
HAVE TIME TO PAY HER A TITHE OF
THE GRATITUDE AND LOVE I OWE
HER,—MY DEAR SWEET MO-
THER,—I DEDICATE THESE
FEW BRIEF INCIDENTS
OF MY ARMY LIFE.

JULY, 1889.   SEPTIMA M. COLLIS.

LIST OF ILLUSTRATIONS.

	PAGE
Septima M. Collis . . . *Frontispiece*	
A Few of our Zouaves in Camp. Taken in the field, 1863	17
Camp of 114th Penna. Vols. (Collis Zouaves) near Culpeper, Va., 1863-4	29
An Officers' Mess, Cook, and Chambermaid—Collis Zouaves, 1863-4	33
Genl. George G. Meade, Commanding Army of the Potomac. Taken in the field, 1863-4	39
Genl. Grant and Staff—City Point, 1864-5. Taken in the field	49
The Field Line and Staff of our Regiment. Taken in front of Petersburg, Va.—Before the fight	53
After the Battle of Petersburg, Va., April, 1865	57

A WOMAN'S WAR RECORD.

By Mrs. General Charles H. T. Collis.

I have no hesitation in calling what I am about to write a "war record," for my life was "twice in jeopardy," as will be seen later on, and I served faithfully as a volunteer, though without compensation, during the entire war of the Rebellion. It is true I was not in the ranks, but I was at the front, and perhaps had a more continuous experience of army life during those four terribly eventful years than any other woman of the North. Born in Charleston, S. C., my sympathies were naturally with the South, but on December 9, 1861, I became a *Union* woman by marrying a Northern soldier in Philadelphia. The romance which resulted in this desertion to the enemy would perhaps interest the reader, yet I do not propose to tell it; for I am sure the very realistic life which it enabled me to experience for three winters in camp at army headquarters will interest him more. My first commander was Gen. Nathaniel P. Banks, to whom I reported on December 11, 1861, at Frederick, Md., where my bridegroom was then a captain of an independent company, which he named and equipped as "Zouaves d'Afrique." The army being in winter quarters, a general disposition prevailed among officers and men to make the season pass merrily. Though the war had by this time assumed serious proportions and the battle of Bull Run had been fought, yet there were many who still believed that the counsels of peace and forbearance would prevail and that the conflict would be of short duration; and this I remember was the daily theme of discussion. Frederick had become a garrisoned town, every train bringing troops and supplies; army wagons and their four-mule teams had possession of the streets, while the sidewalks and shop windows were monopolized by the volunteer officers in their bright buttons and gold lace, who permitted themselves to be disturbed only by the appearance of a pretty face, or by the steady tread of the patrol with their white gloves and polished rifles. My apartments in Frederick consisted of two very modest third-story rooms, sparsely furnished, with the use of a kitchen, at a cheap rent, for we neither of us had any money; yet we indulged in the luxury of the best cook in the army, no other than Nunzio Finelli (one of our zouaves), who was afterwards the steward of the Union League of Philadelphia, and a renowned restaurateur in the same city. Finelli was then a very young man, with a face as handsome as the famous "Neapolitan boy" in the picture, and a voice as sweet and sympathetic as Brignoli's. A most obliging disposition and a fondness for operatic music made him therefore a great acquisition to our little household,—and many an omelette soufflé was first beaten into snowflakes, while the dulcet and plaintive notes of *Ah che la morte* or *Spirito gentil*, reaching the street, detained the spellbound passers-by; and sometimes when his friend and compatriot, Constantino Calarisi (another zouave), joined him in the kitchen, we were treated to a duet which even Patti would have applauded, for they were both very remarkable singers. Poor Finelli! a few months later a bullet at the battle of Cedar Mountain terribly disfigured him, and when I next saw him the shape of his injured nose reminded me of the inhabitants of the Ghetto.

That winter of 1861–2 will be remembered in Frederick till those who enjoyed its " spirit-stirring drum and piercing fife " by day and its " sound of revelry by night " have passed away. There were the swell Bostonians of the Second Massachusetts Regiment, the Hortons, Shaw, Quincy, Choate, and others whose names but not their handsome faces now escape me, and whose waltzing was as gallant then as was their fighting afterwards; and there were the jovial roysterers of " the Twelfth," who from Colonel Fletcher Webster (Daniel's son) down to the humblest subaltern could find in every deed of mischief "a hand to resolve," "a hand to contrive," and a "hand to execute"; and, above all, giving license and encouragement to the playful side of the soldier's life, but presiding over it with a dignity which would brook no violation of discipline or decorum, was the urbane and genial General Banks. Among the ladies who spent the winter with us were Mrs. Banks, Mrs. Holabird, Mrs. Abercrombie, Mrs. Copeland, and Mrs. Scheffler, the wife of one of those German staff officers who had come over to teach our officers the art of war, but who went back home with improved educations. Mrs. Scheffler was a charming woman, thoroughly *naïve*, but could not speak a word of English, and depended much upon me as her interpreter. Upon one occasion, in General Banks' presence, she was fluently expressing to me her views in very complimentary terms regarding his personal appearance, when, to her horror, the General, laughing heartily, thanked her in a very excellent specimen of her native tongue, and we then learned for the first time, and to our discomfiture, that the General was, besides his other accomplishments, an excellent German scholar. Of those ladies who were residents of Frederick and contributed to the general joy, I remember the names of Cooper, Maltby, Schley, McPherson, Goldsborough, and Shriver. There were dress parades of regiments and imposing reviews of brigades and divisions whenever the weather would permit, and to these we women cantered in the saddle, and stood beside the generals while the troops marched by in their picturesque uniforms to splendid music, for at this time every regiment had its special uniform and a brass band, all of which had changed when I witnessed the grand review in Washington at the close of the war, where all were dressed in blue, regiments had been thinned down to companies, and bands of music were few and far between. It seems to me that every Union citizen of Frederick gave a ball or some other entertainment that winter, and many of the regiments returned the courtesy by such improvised hospitality as the scanty accommodations of the camp would afford.

Even thus early in the campaign I came near losing my life. While crossing a ford of the Monocacy River in a light wagon which my husband was driving, we suddenly became aware that the heavy rains had raised the stream to a torrent, and, it being almost dark, we lost our way in mid stream. If you have never been in a wagon in a river when the water became so deep that your horse commenced to swim, you can have no proper appreciation of my sensations. To this day I hardly know how we escaped, but I remember the soldiers on the far-off bank of the stream shouting to us and preparing to leap in to our rescue when our wagon should overturn, which seemed inevitable. It kept its equilibrium, however, and our horse was wheeled around and found a footing, where we remained until the gallant boys in blue waded waist high to our relief.

The *pièce de résistance* of the season, in the way of amusement, was a ball given by Colonel and Mrs. Maltby, who lived in the suburbs of the town. The Colonel, if I remember rightly, then commanded a Maryland regiment or brigade. Their very large and well appointed residence was admirably adapted to gratify the desire of our hostess to make the occasion a memorable one; the immense hall served as the ballroom; the staircases afforded ample sitting room for those who did not participate in, or desired to rest from, the merry whirl, while the ante-rooms presented the most bountiful opportunities of quenching thirst or appeasing appetite. I shall never forget one little French lieutenant who divided his time with precise *ir*regularity between the dance and the punch-bowl, and whose dangling sabre, in its revolutions in the waltz, left as many impressions upon friends as it ever did upon foes; yet it had the happy effect of giving the gentleman and his partner full possession of the field, whenever he could prevail upon some enterprising spinster to join him in cutting a swath through the crowd. Perhaps never did grim War appear to smooth his wrinkled front and yield himself to the *divertissement* of the hour as he did in this charming town in that memorable winter, yet he was really marshalling his hosts for the deadly combat which was to open in the spring. Alas! how soon it came! On Washington's birthday, by express command of President Lincoln (who was chafing under the tardiness of our generals), the army of which my husband and his hundred zouaves were a part, crossed the Potomac River at Harper's Ferry, and we poor women, who would willingly have followed, were ordered home.

Extraordinary as it may appear, I did not fully realize that we were in the midst of a great war until I returned to Philadelphia. In camp the constant round of pleasurable excitement and the general belief that hostilities would be of short duration presented a bright picture without a sombre shadow, and as we bade our loved ones adieu we had few misgivings for their safe return. But at home all was bustle and excitement; a dozen large stores on Chestnut Street had become recruiting stations; public meetings were being held every night to encourage enlistment; politicians were shouting: "On to Richmond!"; young girls were declaring they would never engage themselves to a man who refused to fight for his country, and the fife and drum were heard morning, noon, and night. Yes, indeed, we realized what war meant then much more than we had when among the light-hearted soldiers in the field. The Girard House had, for the time being, been converted from a fashionable hotel into a vast workshop, where the jingle of the sewing-machine and the chatter of the sewing girl, daytime, nighttime, and

Sundays gave evidence that the government was in earnest. Every woman who could use her needle found employment, and those who did not need compensation worked almost as assiduously. About this time some well meaning woman discovered that General Havelock had provided his troops in India with a cotton cap-cover and neck-protector to shield them from the sun of the tropics, and the manufacture of "havelocks" became the ruling mania of the hour. The sewing societies made nothing but havelocks; the shop windows were full of them, and the poor fellows in the army were so inundated with them that those who had the fewest relatives and sweethearts were much the best off.

Vague rumors reached Philadelphia in the early summer of 1862 that General Banks' army had had several day's severe fighting with Stonewall Jackson, and had been defeated, and the tension to which our nerves were wrought in our restless anxiety for fuller news was terrible. Upon one of those ever memorable days I had great difficulty in procuring my favorite newspaper, and was compelled to gather what meagre intelligence I could from other sources. It was not until some time afterwards that I learned that the newspaper had been purposely kept from me. It contained a message from General Banks himself to the Secretary of War, in which he said "Captain Collis and his company of Zouaves d'Afrique were taken prisoners," while an enterprising correspondent of the same paper reported that they had been "cut to pieces." My husband, however, turned up all right. He had covered the retreat of the army, and, being cut off by the enemy, found his way with his zouaves through the mountains of West Virginia to the Upper Potomac. My friends—and thank Heaven I had some good and tried ones (among them a judge of the Supreme Court of the State, whose portrait will always find as choice a place in my home as his memory does in my heart)—brought me the glad intelligence at midnight, and shortly afterwards Mr. Collis was ordered to Philadelphia to increase his command from a company to a regiment. Thus sooner than I expected, my camp life was resumed; but instead of Frederick, Md., with its dances and routes, I found my husband hard at work enlisting men in the city in the morning, and drilling them in Germantown in the afternoon, where he had a charming camp, which he retained until, with a thousand men, early in August of the same year, he once more returned to the field. Antietam,

Fredericksburg, Burnside's muddy march, now came on in quick succession, and my husband was kept so busy with his enlarged command, that although he gladly allowed others a leave of absence, he hesitated to leave the front himself. The suspense in these days was something dreadful—at times, letters arrived quite regularly, and then there followed the long silence and the great anxiety, for we knew when our letters failed us that "the army was moving." Things were very expensive too, especially the necessaries of life; common muslin, I remember, which is now ten cents a yard, then cost a dollar, and the pay of an officer was very small with gold at an enormous premium, so that after he had paid for his "mess" and his servant there was little left for his family at home, though he sent them every dollar he could spare.

A FEW OF OUR ZOUAVES IN CAMP. TAKEN IN THE FIELD, 1863.

What better illustration of the abnormal condition of society in those days can be given than a statement of the fact that my daughter was born on September 25, 1862, and that her father, although within twelve hours' reach of us, did not see her until June, 1863;—and he would not have seen her then, but that he was brought home, it was believed, to die. Careful nursing and desperate fighting by myself and one or two faithful allies restored him soon to health, and he returned to the front,—to find himself at twenty-five years of age in command of a brigade. This promotion was of course gratifying to my pride, but how much more did I value it when I learned that brigade commanders could have their wives with them in camp during the winter, while the unfortunate officers below that rank could not. Yet with all my joy at

God's mercy to me, some days came to me laden with great sorrow. My brother, David Cardoza Levy, a handsome, gallant lieutenant in the Southern army commanded by General Bragg, was about this time killed at the battle of Murfreesborough; seen by his companions to fall, his remains were never afterwards found, though General Rosecrans, to oblige my husband, made every effort to discover them. He lies to-day, God only knows where.

"Without a grave, unknelled, uncoffined, and unknown."

This was the horrible episode of the civil war to me, and although I had many relatives and hosts of friends serving under the Confederate flag all the time, I never fully realized the fratricidal character of the conflict until I lost my idolized brother Dave of the Southern army one day, and was nursing my Northern husband back to life the next.

I very often went to Washington while the Army of the Potomac was lying along the Rappahannock River, and my husband would manage to run up for a few hours to see me. On one of these visits I was presented to President Lincoln, and had a private audience. I shall never forget that wonderful man, and the pressure of the immense hand which grasped mine, so fervent, true, and hearty was his manner. I was very young, and was dressed in such height of fashion as my means afforded—and how strange that fashion seems to me a quarter of a century later. It was forenoon, and yet my out-of-door costume consisted of a pale-pearl silk dress, trimmed with cherry color, immense hoops, and a long train, such as is now very rarely worn even in a ballroom; a black lace shawl, and a little pearl-colored bonnet, with a white illusion veil tied in a tremendous bow under my chin. There were no bustles in those days, except the one worn under the back-hair to support the chignon, which was more commonly called the "waterfall," and though our foreheads were innocent of bangs or crimps, yet, equally absurd, we twisted our hair around pliable little cushions, which were known as rats and mice. What would a tailor-made girl think if she ran across such an outfit on Fifth Avenue to-day? Mr. Lincoln wore a dress suit, I remember, his swallow-tailed coat being a terrible misfit, and it puzzled me very much to tell whether his shirt-collar was made to stand up or to turn down—it was doing a little of both. He was entirely at his ease, and impressed me as being pleased with the diversion which my visit gave him. He referred in complimentary terms to my husband's services, and to the requests of his superior officers for his promotion to Brigadier-General, adding, in a quaint and earnest way, "but he is too young." I replied promptly: "He is not too young to be killed in the service, and make me a widow." "Well," said he, with the *bonhomie* of a courtier, "you would have no trouble in finding promotion *then*," which, for Mr. Lincoln, was, I presume, quite a flirtatious remark. Perhaps he thought that, under the circumstances, I might agree with Madame de Sévigné, who said (with great provocation, it is true): "Would to God we were born widows." While we were thus chatting pleasantly, the door-keeper handed him a card with a woman's name upon it, and whispered a few words to the President as he was putting on his eye-glasses.

Mr. Lincoln uttered a long and agonizing sigh—perhaps I should call it a groan,—and then, turning to me, in a tone of voice as full of sadness as, a moment before it had been full of mirth, said: "This poor woman's son is to be shot to-morrow." I confess I was so overpowered by his distress that I had hardly the strength to speak, but, by way of comfort, I ventured the opinion that I presumed such things were inevitable in time of war. "Yes," said he, slowly and pensively, as he threw his head far back and pressed his brow with his hand, "that's so; but there's so many on 'em, so many on 'em." Of course this brought our interview to a close, and I gave way to the broken-hearted mother, who, I am sure, left that great presence as full of hope as I did of love and reverence for this remarkable man. I never again saw him until I met him at City Point,

Va., a few days before the assassination.

In the autumn of 1863 I received a telegram that my husband was very ill with pneumonia, in camp near Culpeper, Va. Major-General Meade happened to be in Philadelphia at the time, and I took the telegram to him and begged him to give me a pass to visit the army at once. There existed at that time a positive order against ladies going to the front, but General Meade, whom I had known intimately for many years, made an exception in my case, and with his autograph passport I started at once, leaving my baby to the tender care of devoted friends (the Misses C——), whose kindness in this emergency I shall never forget. But my troubles only commenced when I reached Alexandria. Such a place as it was there—a perfect Bedlam; all confusion; no hotel (the one where Col. Ellsworth had been shot being then used as a hospital or storehouse); the muddy streets thronged with lazy negroes and affrighted cattle; wounded soldiers staring with amazement at the young woman in civilized attire who seemed to have dropped among them from the clouds, I suppose; and drunken recruits and conscripts singing ribald songs. But for the ever-present call of duty which impelled me to go to the bedside of my suffering husband, I would have turned back, as Gen. Meade told me I would; but my eyes and my heart were looking southerly, and to the south I was determined to go at any risk. My life has not been without adventure: I have crossed the Atlantic a dozen times; have been in a collision in mid-ocean, and will carry to my grave the recollection of the agonizing cries of the drowning victims; have stood upon the crater of Vesuvius during an eruption; have lived in a railroad construction camp on the Rocky Mountains, with its ruffians, its gamblers, and its Chinamen; have made an ascent in a balloon; have seen a Cinnamon bear shot within fifty yards of me; have for nights slept upon the bare floor of an isolated log-hut amidst the geysers of the Yellowstone; have had a volley of rifle-balls whistle around my ears; yet never in my experience did my heart throb as nervously as when I stood alone in the streets of Alexandria waiting to be lifted into a cattle-train which was soon to start for the army at Brandy Station, near Culpeper. The officers who had charge of the train remonstrated with me, and endeavored to detain me with the promise that, if I waited an hour or so, I should have a special car. Little did they know the woman they were dealing with. I was even then very decisive and quite skeptical, traits which were not so well developed as they are to-day. In the first place, I knew the necessity for my immediate presence in camp, and, in the second, I did n't believe a word in their promise that I would be any better off by waiting. So, armed with Gen. Meade's pass and a determined and perhaps petulant will, I was lifted into a dirty cattle-car, and sat, not on a lounge, but on the head of a barrel amidst the soldiers, who were drinking, smoking, and singing. They were not in any way rude, but their guns were all loaded and while they slept and snored at my feet, I feared a sudden movement would set off a gun, and that of course *I* would be the victim. I did n't sleep a wink; the night was very cold but I was warmly wrapped up and cared less for my discomfort than I did for the snail's pace at which we were travelling. It was the gray of the dawn when we reached Brandy Station, where a staff-officer with an ambulance met me and took me a long ride to the house of Mr. Yancey, where I found my husband in a comfortable room, being well cared for. For the second time in twelve months I became an army nurse, but it took all my skill and watching to counteract the blunders of the so-called army surgeons. The day after my arrival one of these incompetents blistered his patient's chest until it was raw, and then made a plaster of cold cream, which he carried in the open air from his tent to the sick chamber, a distance of several hundred yards, on a freezing cold night, and clapped it on the patient's burning and lacerated flesh. It must have been like the shock of an electric battery, for the air was instantly blue with language which never before or since have I heard pass my husband's lips, and he himself was in the middle of the floor, sick as he was, hurling the plaster into the doctor's face. What part I took in the scene it becomes me better to leave to the imagination of those who know me, than to set down in print. Let it suffice that his services were dispensed with, and General French sent us the medical director of the corps, who soon had his patient fit for duty, and I returned to Philadelphia. Yancey, by the by, was an awful rebel. He prided himself that he had never been to Washington or Richmond and had barely heard of New York and Philadelphia. "I 've allas lived right 'round Culpeppa Sah" was his daily boast, and his only religion seemed to be a hatred for the Yan-

CAMP OF 114TH PENNA. VOLS. (COLLIS ZOUAVES) NEAR CULPEPER, VA., 1863-4.

kees. It was therefore very unfortunate that, upon the execution of the order that all persons within the lines of the army should be vaccinated, some impure vaccine matter, by an unforeseen accident, found its way into Yancey's blood, or else that he caught cold, for he had a terrible arm and was laid up for weeks, thoroughly convinced that he had been purposely poisoned; and if he is living to-day I don't doubt that he often tells the story of the Yankee effort to take his life.

I next joined the army on January 1, 1864. It was still at Brandy Station, but instead of Yancey's house I found awaiting my arrival the most picturesque home I have ever lived in; it will ever be remembered as one of the brightest surprises of my life. Imagine two ordinary army tents, set close together, one of them for a parlor and dining-room, the other for a bedroom; both having chimneys of mud and stone, presenting fine open fireplaces with *real* mantel-pieces on the inside; the bedstead was of plain pine timber, and the bedding delicious, sweet, clean straw sewed up in sacks, the whole covered with a layer of several brown woollen army blankets; there were, of course, no pillows or pillow-cases, a couple of saddles answered for the one, and I presume imagination had to do service for the other; yet we were supremely happy. I was a soldier, and these were war times, and I prided myself that I could dispense with luxuries and yet be comfortable. [There is no woman who can, better than I, enjoy beautiful surroundings, and who absolutely craves all the exquisite *luxe* that is obtainable, or can sleep more deliciously under the light, warm, silken eider-down, but it is a great satisfaction that these war experiences have fitted me to climb a mountain, sleep upon a bare floor, or ride twenty miles in a rain storm, and overcome situations which, without them, I never would have surmounted.] But it was bitterly cold sometimes that winter in these canvas houses, and I did not dare leave my bed in the mornings until our man, who was maid-of-all-work, built a great big log fire and literally drove us out of bed with the heat. And, oh! what a grandiose parlor did I step into for breakfast the first morning I was there, with its works of art cut from the illustrated newspapers of the day, framed with strips of red flannel, while on my mantel were spread varieties of bonbons imported expressly from Washington to celebrate my arrival. Our table service was of pure tin, washed and burnished with sand and water after every meal, and because our spoons were of the same material our soup was not a jot the less savory; as we seldom indulged in French peas our two-pronged forks answered every purpose, and as I occasionally managed to borrow a table-cloth and sometimes a napkin from our neighbor Yancey, our little *tête-à-tête* dinners were quite *recherché*, considering the surroundings. But my habitation was a gem, worthy a place in any collection of "Happy Homes." When, however, my baby daughter and her nurse joined me I gave up my "open-air" life and returned to the Yancey mansion, where I remained until General Grant, fresh from his marvellous victories in the West, came among us and made preparations for his advance to Richmond.

During this winter the different

AN OFFICERS' MESS, COOK, AND CHAMBERMAID—COLLIS ZOUAVES, 1863-4.

head-quarters were very gay, and we wives who were so fortunate as to be with our husbands, instead of spending our time alone and anxious at home, had plenty of enjoyment. Of course, the officers were constantly inventing new schemes of *divertissement*. What with dinners, balls, reviews, races, and cavalcades, we had few idle moments. I was an excellent and fearless rider, owning my own saddle and *borrowing* my mount. It was no uncommon thing for me to ride from our camp to the head-quarters of General Meade, a distance of twenty miles, and return home to dinner in the evening; and more than once I came to grief, always, of course, through the fault of my horse and not of his rider (?). I pleasantly remember one or two visits to Hon. John Minor Botts and his family, whose residence was within our camp.

It was during this winter that the Fifth Corps, commanded by Major-General Warren, gave a magnificent ball, quite unique as to decorations, etc. The ballroom consisted of several hospital tents, and the banquet hall of another. These were all smoothly floored; there were several bands, so that the music was continuous; highly polished rifles in ornamental groups; bright brass cannon, lots of drums, and a sea of bunting; the whole illuminated with clusters of wax candles and Chinese lanterns. The handsome uniforms of the officers, to say nothing of their handsome faces and figures; the clashing of their sabres, the jingle of their spurs, and the universal expression upon every face and in every gesture to "be merry while we may," made it a scene of enchantment which was to me so novel and so suited to my years and my tastes that I consider it a great privilege to have been a part of it.

Of course I received a great deal of attention. I expected it, and I was not disappointed, and I confess that during those exhilarating hours I don't believe a thought ever entered my mind that many of these splendid fellows were dancing their last waltz, and I am very sure such gloomy forebodings never entered theirs; no, it was

"A very merry, dancing, drinking,
 Laughing, quaffing, and *unthinking* time."

Indeed, it was "unthinking." Well do I remember expressing my sympathy to a very distinguished cavalry general for the loss of his only son; to which the gallant sabreur responded: "Yes, madame, very sad! very sad! he was the last of his race! Do you waltz?" and away he went to the exhilarating music of a dashing galop, leaving all melancholy far behind him. The very superb supper and the waiters, I remember, came from Washington, and an express-train brought an immense number of fashionable people from the North. The costumes of the women were superb, quite as elegant and elaborate as displayed at any similar entertainment in city life. The beautiful Miss Kate Chase was the acknowledged belle of the occasion. The ball did not break up until near morning, and then we poor, tired women, in all our finery, were distributed to our respective tented homes in ambulances and army wagons, and as we meandered through the little canvas villages, with their smouldering fires and "fixed sentinels," the serious aspect of the epoch chased away the merry memory of mirth.

The winter of 1864-5 I passed

at City Point, Va., the head-quarters of General Grant. At first we lived in tents, but later, when my husband became commander of the post, I lived most comfortably in a house. These were the months immediately preceding the close of the war, and were the most interesting, full of excitement and stirring events. I had my little daughter with me, and we occupied a very cosy farm-house, where for the first time in my army life I had female servants, one of whom was an old colored woman I found on the premises, and she did most excellent service as cook and maid-of-all-work. In real Southern style we called her "Aunty" Miranda. Being a particularly crisp, dry winter, I was constantly in the saddle, galloping to the different head-quarters, and stopping on the way now and then to visit Generals Meade, Burnside, Hancock, and other conspicuous men of that day, all of whom I knew well, but, alas! nothing of whom now remains but their fame. The army was then lying in the trenches around Petersburg. General Meade's camp was beautifully situated some miles from City Point upon a knoll which had once been a pine grove, but the timber had been cut down and up for firewood, leaving nothing but a barren array of tents. Upon his staff were the hard-working Seth Williams; General Hunt, who I saw recently at Gettysburg, very little changed in appearance, and not at all changed in genial manner and urbanity, yet who has since joined his departed comrades; Colonel Biddle, of Philadelphia, ever in good spirits; the gallant Captain Cadwalader, of the same city, and young George Meade then a mere lad. General Burnside was encamped in quite a picturesque

GENL. GEORGE G. MEADE, COMMANDING ARMY OF THE POTOMAC. TAKEN IN THE FIELD, 1863–4.

ever-green enclosure, and was surrounded by a staff carefully selected from the choicest of Rhode-Island's sons, all of whom had distinguished themselves on many hard-fought fields; and the superb Hancock, still suffering occasionally from his Gettysburg wound, had possession of a farmhouse, where, from what I could see, he was well cared for by two young Philadelphians, Bingham and Parker, of his staff. When my husband's duties prevented his accompanying me I frequently took these long rides with an orderly, well mounted and armed, and more than once lost my way and got outside the lines. In those days, however, I had no fear, for I had a notion that if captured, being a Southern woman, I would have found myself among friends. On one particular road I was several times stopped by a Union picket, who demanded the countersign, which I, of course, did not possess, but I paid little heed to the demand, excepting to make some laughing remark to the effect that "I commanded a brigade," or was "Commander of the Post," and always dashed on. My orderly, however (David Smith, of the 114th Pennsylvania Volunteers), took alarm and admonished me that I was running the risk of being shot by some stupid sentinel, who might take me for a female spy, and as he peached on me also to my commanding officer, I got a gentle reprimand, which compelled me to abandon my favorite turnpike in the future. Our *cuisine* at City Point was superb. Being the rendezvous of the sutlers and caterers of the army, we naturally had the best the Northern markets could supply, and, of course, an abundance of turtle, fish, and oysters from the James River. Mr.

Maltby, now the proprietor of the Lafayette Hotel in Philadelphia, was enterprising enough to erect a hotel, which was well kept and well patronized, and the camp was full of restaurants and oyster-houses, but the selling of intoxicating beverages was under such strict surveillance that there was rarely a case of drunkenness, and when there was, the punishment of one night in the "bull pen," presided over by Captain Savage, was worse than a month in a house of correction.

Speaking of the "bull pen," that was a horrid place. Originally the "precincts of the jail" had been confined to the four walls of a church, but as the number of prisoners increased, it became necessary to make a large enclosure with a high board fence, but with only the sky (and frequently a very damp sky) for a roof. In this pigpen, *I* call it, in rain and snow and frost I have seen hundreds, perhaps thousands, of men huddled together without a particle of shelter or protection from the elements—perhaps there was no help for it,—at all events its horror and its odor sicken me to think of, even a quarter of a century later, and as I don't like to write about it I will turn to something pleasanter.

Returning one evening, just at dusk, from one of our long horseback rides, Mr. Collis and myself were both very hungry, and a life among soldiers having made me somewhat indifferent to conventionalities, I threw a dozen James-River oysters on the embers of my wood fire, and threw myself on the floor; got Aunty Miranda to furnish us with butter, pepper, and salt; rolled up the sleeves of my riding habit, and was in the act of devouring, while my husband in similar pose, was in the act of opening, the succulent bivalves when I heard a knock at the door, and in response to my " come in," who *should* come in but General and Mrs. Grant, just to make a social call. Consternation is hardly the word to express it. Just to think of it! this was the first time in my grown-up life that I had ever eaten a meal in that position (picnics excepted), and why on earth should General and Mrs. Grant come just at that moment. How I got up and what I did with the oysters I do not know and never shall, but I *do* know that our guests enjoyed the situation heartily, and were good enough to say they envied us, and when we apologized for the tin teapot and pewter spoons which adorned the table for our evening meal, the General said that we were just as well off as he was, which we later found to be the fact when we visited his famous log-cabin (now in Fairmount Park), though before the winter closed we got to be quite luxurious with our white china plates, table-cloths, and even napkins on swell occasions.

My husband was this winter kept busy every day as President of a court-martial which was trying spies and deserters, the latter being in those days, I remember, called "bounty-jumpers," that is, they made it a business to enlist in the North, receive the heavy bounties—which, if I remember rightly, at that time amounted to upwards of a thousand dollars,—and then, when they came to the army, they deserted to the enemy, changed their clothing, and came back as rebels, were sent North, again escaped, reënlisted and received another bounty, and so on. It was a regular business, and General Grant became so incensed when he discovered it that he determined to end it. As the result of the trials the leaders were all shot, and the others sentenced to long terms of imprisonment, and I believe the demoralization ceased. Still it was terrible to see these poor wretches day after day manacled with ball-and-chain, going in and out of the court-room; my heart bled for them, it is true, yet I was told that the safety of the army depended upon their summary punishment. There were some executions by hanging, also, that winter, for crimes of a more heinous character, in several instances of negro teamsters, and although, in my many rides, I tried to avoid the sight of the gallows, they *would* occasionally loom up. After each execution they were kept standing, I suppose, as a warning to other malefactors. Among the deserters who were tried were many young foreigners who could not speak a word of English, but as they were merely the tools of the leaders, who robbed them of their bounties, they were more leniently dealt with.

One of the incidents of this winter was a visit I made to Dutch-Gap Canal, which was nearly completed; and while looking across the river at the enemy, our party was vigorously fired at by the Southern artillery, forcing us (there were one or two other ladies in the party) to huddle ourselves with the soldiers in a bomb-proof until the firing ceased. We then scampered at a lively gait for our horses, and were out of reach as fast as their hoofs would carry us. I was quite used, however, to artillery-firing by this time, though I had never until then been in any danger. Frequently, when I heard cannonading, I rode out beyond the Avery House to an eminence overlooking the town of Petersburg, and within perhaps two miles of it, and for hours watched the "bombs bursting in air," and saw wagon-loads of earth literally ploughed up by cannon-balls. Upon another momentous occasion, all the ladies in camp were peremptorily ordered on board a steamboat, which immediately steamed down the river out of harm's way, among the number being Mrs. Grant herself. A rebel gunboat or ram, or something of the kind, had forced its way down the river, and was throwing shells right and left at a great rate, creating much alarm. The firing lasted all day, and when we returned we found that General Grant's headquarters, on the bank of the river, had been turned into a fortress, and was mounted with heavy guns. It appeared that one of our monitors had retreated upon the approach of the enemy's vessel, and I have often heard my husband relate that he had never seen General Grant lose his temper excepting upon that occasion, when he soundly berated the naval officer for not blowing up his ship or scuttling her in the channel in preference to endangering the lives and valuable stores at City Point.

In the midst of these stirring events a terrible anxiety overcame me—my child commenced ailing, and her disease rapidly developed into scarlet-fever. What, however, with the skilful treatment of Dr. Dalton, of Boston, then a medical director in the army, and of an excellent army nurse, in a few weeks she was out of danger, but remained in delicate health until I returned to Philadelphia. I mention this circumstance because it prolonged my stay in the army long after all other ladies had departed for home, hence my unexpected experiences at the renewal of hostilities in the spring of 1865.

GENL. GRANT AND STAFF—CITY POINT, 1864-5. TAKEN IN THE FIELD.

It was on the memorable second of April, 1865 (Sunday), about daylight, that my husband asked me whether I would not like to jump on my horse and go to the front to see a battle, which he felt sure would take place that day; he assured me that whatever might befall *him*, I would not be in the slightest danger. It was a damp, disagreeable morning, and, as my daughter was only convalescing, I said: " No, I am afraid to leave the child." Well! I slept on; when suddenly I heard such a roar of cannon as made every timber in my little house tremble and vibrate from cellar to roof. I dressed quickly, for my utter ignorance of what was going on made me imagine all kinds of terrible things, and the hospital nurse only served further to demoralize me, exclaiming every moment: " I am not afraid, but we are not safe here." From my front-door I distinctly saw the flash of the cannon; and twenty-four eventful years have not effaced from my memory those bursts of vivid lightning and the continuous roar of angry thunder, while the whole air was black with smoke from the burning tobacco-warehouses in Petersburg.

You can imagine that this was a day to me of great anxiety. I looked out upon my husband's camp, and found it was deserted. He had slipped away with his brigade, gone to the front, and I had not known it. He preferred that I should not know it. City Point had but a few soldiers left to protect the government stores, and General Grant's head-quarters were occupied only by his Adjutant-General, Colonel Bowers, and Mr. President Lincoln.* I got immediately into the saddle, and, with my trusty orderly, was not long in placing myself within view of the fighting. The

* See note, page 78.

cannonading was dying out, but the small-arms kept up their fusillade; the black column of smoke was still steadily ascending, several houses were in flames, and the whole town seemed to be enshrouded in a white vapor cloud, common, I suppose, to all battle-fields. Ambulances were coming to the rear laden with the unfortunate wounded, and some who were *not* wounded, I regret to say, were also facing the wrong way; and of these cowards I was deadly afraid, always changing my course to avoid them. I could learn nothing more of our brigade, than that they had stormed the works early in the morning, had been successful, and were still holding them. Evening came! Night came! and in the shadow of the doomed city, with its glare of smouldering ruins lit up occasionally by the flash from a cannon or the explosion of a shell, sat two anxious figures on horseback, hoping against hope for some word of comfort. Finally, I gave it up, and returned to my sick child. Was I widowed? Was my husband lying in the trenches suffering from some horrible wound, and I not near him? Oh, what an anxious night! Colonel Bowers and Mr. Lincoln were still at City Point. I could only learn from them that, so far, our army had been victorious, but they knew nothing of what I wanted most to hear. The few men in camp were in high glee, cheering and singing and lighting bonfires, but my little household knew not whether to be joyous or sad. Ours was an awful suspense, which seemed an eternity. Daylight found me in the saddle again, and in half an hour I was at the house of good old Mrs. Bott, whose property, near Petersburg, my husband had always carefully protected,

THE FIELD LINE AND STAFF OF OUR REGIMENT. TAKEN IN FRONT OF PETERSBURG, VA.—BEFORE THE FIGHT.

and from whom I frequently purchased butter and eggs. If my husband was alive and well, I knew he would stop here on his return, just as I knew he would expect to find me there awaiting him. Here I learned that our brigade had made a desperate charge, and that Mr. Collis' own regiment, with which he led the assault, had suffered severely, three of his favorite officers having been killed, Captain Eddy and Lieutenants Cunningham and Marion, all gallant soldiers who had risen from the ranks of his old "independent" company, and all of whom on that fatal Sunday morning had every reason to believe that the war was substantially over, and that they would soon return to their homes. Poor Captain Eddy I saw just before he died; the bullet had torn away a portion of his skull, and he never recovered consciousness. Oh, how sickening, in these days of peace, come the memories of those ensanguined hours! Learning the direction in which the brigade was returning, I rode on at a rapid pace, my young heart full of gratitude for God's mercy to me while others had been made to so severely suffer, when suddenly, just as the troops came within sight, to my horror I found myself in the midst of a shower of bullets, whizzing thick and fast around my ears like the buzzing of angry wasps. Only the presence of mind of my faithful orderly saved my life. "Follow me," he cried, and, in less time than it takes to write it, we and our horses were in a ravine or quarry at the road-side, where we remained until the firing had ceased. Was it the enemy? Was I to be captured? After all, were these rebels and not Union soldiers whom I had seen as I looked through the strip of trees which separated us? They proved to be my husband's own men, firing into the timber to empty their loaded muskets, and thus save the trouble of drawing the loads. I will not repeat the elegant " army " language which my spouse used on that occasion, but I assure you the firing promptly ceased, and he galloped up to receive my congratulations on his safety. But he was a sorry sight, literally covered from head to foot with cakes of mud—his high top-boots full of it, and his hair matted with it. His beautiful white horse, which he could not take with him into the trenches, was the only clean thing in the entire command. The brigade had lain literally " in the last ditch " the whole night, and the ditch, he told me, had six inches of water in it.

Quite a humorous and yet pathetic incident occurred during our ride back. We overtook a negro soldier very badly wounded in the arm, but marching proudly erect to City Point, still carrying his gun, cartridge-box, and haversack. Mr. Collis told him to throw these encumbrances away, but he refused, and then upon being ordered to do so, begged most earnestly to be permitted to retain them, because, as he expressed it, "I don't want de fellows at de hospital to mistake me for a teamster." We were soon home and in camp, and having eaten a hearty breakfast, Mr. Collis donned his only remaining suit of clothes and by direction of General Grant started for Richmond, which had been evacuated by Jefferson Davis and was then being entered by our troops. A little party of distinguished sight-seers had just come down from the North, little anticipating the exciting scenes in store

AFTER THE BATTLE OF PETERSBURG, VA., APRIL, 1865.

for them; they consisted of "Prince" John Van Buren and his charming daughter, Mrs. Stoughton and General and Colonel Stoughton, Mr. Arthur Leary, Mrs. Paran Stevens, Miss Reed, and some others whose names I regret to have forgotten. It did not take long to supply the entire party with horses, saddles, and side-saddles, and getting aboard a steamer in the harbor, we went as far up the river as the torpedoes would permit (I think the place was called Rockett's), and then rode with our cavalry escort right into the city of Richmond, though the last mile was in a drenching rain, which wet us all to the skin. The capital of the Confederacy really did seem evacuated, and save for the fact that every now and then there was a slamming of a door or shutter with an unmistakable emphasis of the contempt in which we were held by the lady on the other side, one would have supposed that the inhabitants had entirely abandoned it. Riding at a quick canter, we did not rein up until we reached the residence of Mr. Davis himself, where we found some of the colored servants still in possession, who received us with civility and helped us to dry our clothes. Having done this (to a certain extent), we rode around to the Capitol, the horrible and filthy Libby Prison, the burning district, and other places of interest and returned home in the evening, quite proud of the fact that we were the first Northern women to enter the beleaguered city.

While the people of the North were celebrating with guns and brass bands and bunting the capture of Petersburg and the evacuation of Richmond, while every loyal city was dressed in its holiday attire, and its inhabitants were intoxicated with joy, the chain of events at City Point "all of which I saw, and part of which I was," kept me still within the gloom and shadow of the war, while those removed from its actual presence were merry-making in the brilliance of the victory. City Point became one vast hospital for suffering humanity. As far as the eye could reach from the door-step of my humble home, the plain was dotted with tents which were rapidly filled with wounded men, Northern and Southern, white and black without distinction; army surgeons, and volunteer physicians just arrived, were kept sleeplessly at work; hospital nurses and the good Samaritans of the Sanitary Commission, laden with comforts for the sick and wounded, were passing to and fro, and amidst them all strode the tall gaunt figure of Abraham Lincoln, his moistened eyes even more eloquent than the lips, which had a kindly word of cheer for every sufferer. I had met Mr. Lincoln a few days before the crisis of which I am writing arrived, and was glad to know that he remembered me. My husband, who was present, asked him *en passant* how long he intended to remain with the army; "Well," said Mr. Lincoln, with as much caution as though he were being interviewed for publication, "I am like the western pioneer who built a log cabin. When he commenced he did n't know how much timber he would need, and when he had finished, he did n't care how much he had used up"; and then added with a merry laugh: "So you see I came down among you without any definite plans, and when I go home I sha'n't regret a moment I have spent with you."

About this time a very touching incident occurred, which serves, as well as any anecdote yet told, to illustrate that "charity for all and malice toward none" were not mere "words" with Abraham Lincoln, but that they were a part of his very nature and being.

It is a true story, told only once, in the initial number of *Once a Week*, and I will insert it here in my husband's own language.

LINCOLN'S MAGNANIMITY.

BY CHAS. H. T. COLLIS.

During the few eventful days which immediately preceded the fall of Richmond, Abraham Lincoln tarried at City Point, Va., awaiting the news from Grant, Meade, and Sheridan, who were pulverizing Lee's right wing, while Sherman was hurrying his victorious column toward Savannah. Time hung wearily with the President, and as he walked through the hospitals or rode amid the tents, his rueful countenance bore sad evidence of the anxiety and anguish which possessed him. Presently, however, squads, and then hundreds, and later thousands of prisoners, of high and low degree, came from the front, and we all began to realize, from what we saw of their condition, and what the prisoners themselves told us, that the Confederacy was crumbling to pieces.

Among the captured were Generals Ewell, Custis Lee, and Barringer, who became the guests of myself and wife, I being at the time Commandant of the Post, and right well did they enjoy the only good square meal that had gladdened their eyes and their palates for many a long day.

General Barringer, of North Carolina, was the first to arrive. He was a polished, scholarly, and urbane gentleman, scrupulously regarding the parole I had exacted from him, and deeply sensible and appreciative of my poor efforts to make him comfortable.

Hearing that Mr. Lincoln was at City Point, the General one day begged me to give him an opportunity to see him as he walked or rode through the camp, and happening to spend that evening with the President in the tent of Colonel Bowers, Grant's Adjutant-General, who had remained behind to keep up communication with the armies operating across the James River, I incidentally referred to the request of General Barringer. Mr. Lincoln immediately asked me to present his compliments to the General, and to say he would like very much to see him, whispering to me in his quaint and jocose way:

"Do you know I have never seen a live rebel general in full uniform."

At once communicating the President's wish to General Barringer, I found that officer much embarrassed. He feared I had overstepped the bounds of propriety in mentioning his curiosity to see the Northern President, and that Mr. Lincoln would think him a very impertinent fellow, besides which he was muddy, and tattered, and torn, and not at all presentable.

Reassuring him as best I could, he at last sought those embellishments which a whisk, a blacking-brush, and a comb provided, and we walked over to headquarters, where we found the President in high feather, listening to the cheerful messages from Grant at the front.

I formally presented General Barringer, of North Carolina, to the President of the United States, and Mr. Lincoln extended his hand, warmly welcomed him, and bade him be seated. There was, however, only one chair vacant when the President arose, and this the Southerner very politely declined to take.

This left the two men facing each other in the centre of the tent, the tall form of Mr. Lincoln almost reaching the ridge-pole. He slowly removed his eye-glasses, looked the General over from head to foot, and then in a slow, meditative, and puzzled manner inquired:

"Barringer? Barringer? from North Carolina? Barringer of North Carolina? General, were you ever in Congress?"

"No, Mr. Lincoln, I never was," replied the General.

"Well, I thought not; I thought my memory could n't be so much at fault. But there *was* a Barringer in Congress with me, and from your State too!"

"That was my brother, sir," said Barringer.

Up to this moment the hard face of the President had that thoughtful, troubled expression with which those of us who knew him were only too familiar, but now the lines melted away, and the eyes and the tongue both laughed. I cannot describe the change, though I still see it and shall never forget it. It was like a great sudden burst of sunshine in a rain storm.

"Well! well!" exclaimed the great and good man, burying for the moment all thought of war, its cares, its asperities, and the frightful labor it had imposed upon him; his heart welling up only to the joyous reminiscence which the meeting brought to him.

"Well! well!" said he; "do you know

that that brother of yours was my chum in Congress. Yes, sir, we sat at the same desk and ate at the same table. He was a Whig and so was I. He was my chum, and I was very fond of him. And you are his brother, eh? Well! well! shake again." And once more in the pressure of his great big hand his heart went out to this man in arms against the government, simply because his brother had been his chum and was a good fellow.

A couple more chairs by this time had been added to the scant furniture of the Adjutant-General's tent, and the conversation drifted from Mr. Lincoln's anecdotes of the pleasant hours he and Barringer had spent together, to the war, thence to the merits of military and civil leaders, North and South, illustrated here and there by some appropriate story, entirely new, full of humor and sometimes of pathos.

Several times the General made a movement to depart, fearing he was availing himself too lavishly of Mr.

Lincoln's affability, but each time was ordered to keep his seat, the President remarking that they were both prisoners, and he hoped the General would take some pity upon him and help him to talk about the times when they were both their own masters, and had n't everybody criticising and abusing them.

Finally, however, General Barringer arose, and was bowing himself out, when Mr. Lincoln once more took him by the hand almost affectionately, placed another hand upon his shoulder, and inquired quite seriously:

"Do you think I can be of any service to you?"

Not until we had all finished a hearty laugh at this quaint remark did the President realize the innocent simplicity of his inquiry, and when General Barringer was able to reply that "If anybody can be of service to a poor devil in my situation, I presume you are the man," Mr. Lincoln drew a blank card from his vest pocket, adjusted his glasses, turned up the wick of the lamp, and sat down at General Bowers' desk with all the serious earnestness with which you would suppose he had attached his name to the emancipation proclamation.

This was, however, all assumed. He was equipping himself and preparing us for one of his little jokes. While writing he kept up a running conversation with General Barringer (who was still standing and wondering) to this effect:

"I suppose they will send you to Washington, and there I have no doubt they will put you in the old Capitol prison. I am told it is n't a nice sort of a place, and I am afraid you won't find it a very comfortable tavern; but I have a powerful friend in Washington—he's the biggest man in the country,—and I believe I have some influence with him when I don't ask too much. Now I want you to send this card of introduction to him, and if he takes the notion he may put you on your parole, or let up on you that way or some other way. Anyhow, it's worth while trying."

And then very deliberately drying the card with the blotter, he held it up to the light and read it to us in about the following words:

"This is General Barringer, of the Southern army. He is the brother of a very dear friend of mine. Can you do any thing to make his detention in Washington as comfortable as possible under the circumstances?

"A. LINCOLN.
"To HON. EDWIN M. STANTON,
   "Secretary of War."

Barringer never uttered a word. I think he made an effort to say "Thank you," or "God bless you," or something of that kind, but he was speechless. We both wheeled about and left the tent.

After walking a few yards, not hearing any footsteps near me, and fearing Barringer had lost his way, I turned back and found this gallant leader of brave men, who had won his stars in a score of battles, "like Niobe, all tears," audibly sobbing and terribly overcome.

He took my arm, and as we walked slowly home he gave voice to as hearty expressions of love for the great Lincoln as have been since uttered by his most devoted and life-long friends.

A few years afterwards I met the General socially in Philadelphia, and we went over this episode in his life, as I have narrated it, and then, for the third time, his eyes filled as he told me how he had wept and wept at "the deep damnation of his taking off."

The "bull pen," of which I have already spoken, was, in these early days of April, so densely packed with prisoners of war that the overflow were permitted to sleep outside the enclosure. Poor fellows, there was little danger of their running away. Such a mass of hungry, unshaven, ragged, and forlorn humanity was never seen before, and will, I hope, never again be seen in our country. No wonder they looked tattered and torn, fighting for days in the trenches, then driven from pillar to post and hunted down till they fell by the road-side from sheer exhaustion; then captured and hurried to City Point, several miles distant, through rain and mud, with no shelter, no food, no any thing, save the little which the Union soldier in mercy and pity could spare from his own scanty supply. In the "bull pen," however, they had plenty of hot *real* coffee (so long a stranger to their lips), and good fresh bread and meat, and after a day's rest they were sent by the boat-load to the North. My husband did his best to provide comfortable quarters for the Confederate officers, and brought Generals Ewell, Barringer, and Custis Lee to our own little house. The two former dined with us upon their arrival, but, if I remember rightly, the latter went right on to Washington. It gave me great pleasure to have these distinguished men as my guests, rebels though they were, and I was glad to have it in my power to show them that there was a disposition to welcome the prodigals' return with the fatted calf. Being quite a *cordon bleu* myself, it was not difficult to present an attractive *menu*, consisting of superb raw oysters, green-turtle soup, a delicious James-River shad, and a fillet of army beef. A bottle of whiskey and another of brandy, and a cup of good black coffee constituted the dinner which, General Barringer was good enough to say, and said it as if he meant it, was the first square meal he had eaten in two years. The General was a charming gentleman, appreciative, tolerant, and resigned. General Ewell was irritable, disappointed, and disposed to be out of humor with every thing and everybody; yet who could blame him in that hour of his culminating misfortunes. The loss of a leg in battle appealed to my sympathy, the loss of station, fortune, and the attainment of his ambition made me pardon his irascibility. Among other things, he could not understand how a Southern woman could espouse the Northern cause simply because she had married a Northerner, but I forced him into a more cheerful mood, I think, when I told him that I had only followed the example of many other Southrons,—I had "gone with my State," mine being the state of matrimony.

General Grant at this time was in pursuit of Lee's retreating army, and my husband's brigade was once more ordered on the march, while I, with my sick child, remained at City

Point. It was not until April 14th that I considered my daughter well enough to travel, and then, without waiting for my husband's return from Appomattox, I started for Philadelphia, taking a steamboat as far as Baltimore. The war was over; my husband was alive and well; my child was recovering; my life was brimful of gladness. With such happy thoughts and in such a mood I reached Baltimore, when I gradually became sensible of an abnormal condition of things, which indicated some fresh outbreak, and I became alarmed. People were hurrying through the streets, groups of men and women were engaged in eager discussion; something had happened. There were no cheers, no music; it was gloom! There had been a *calamity*. What was it? "The President has been murdered," whispered my orderly, who had gone for information, "and nobody can go North to-day." Oh, horror! I had learned to love Mr. Lincoln then, as younger people to-day love to read about him. I had seen him weep, had heard him laugh, had been gladdened by his wit and saddened by his pathos. I had looked up to him as one inspired. How glad I was afterwards to know that his untimely death was the act of a mad fanatic, and that my people who had fought a desperate but unreasonable war had no hand in it.

When I could collect my thoughts I gathered up my sick child and the little comforts I had brought with me to nourish and sustain her on the journey, and took myself to the nearest hotel, where I remained until the authorities permitted me to continue on my way the next morning. Later I was among the sad and silent multitude who witnessed the passing of the funeral cortége up Broad Street, in Philadelphia. There were many joys in my life then which made me the happiest of women, but I could willingly have sacrificed some of them to bring that best of the very best back again into life.

In the middle of May, 1865, I was once more in camp, this time at Arlington Heights, Va., and witnessed the magnificent reviews of Meade's and Sherman's armies on Pennsylvania Avenue, in Washington. I shall never forget the dashing Custer, his sombrero, his flowing red scarf, his long blond hair,—the *beau ideal* of a cavalry leader, as his charger reared and pranced and became almost unmanageable; nor am I likely to forget that, for a better view, I was lifted above the crowd by the strong arms of my escort (I was then quite *petite*), and that at that moment the photograph fiend was on hand and secured the lasting evidence of the fact that I was in the arms of a stalwart man in broad daylight.

The continuous columns of these martial hosts, their victorious cheers, their well-worn uniforms, ribboned battle-flags, fifes, drums, and bands, seemed to give utterance to but a single thought, and that was: "This is the Northern army returning from its victory over the South"; but to-day, as I look back over twenty years of peace and prosperity, I feel that there was victory for the South in the defeat. It cost the lives of many dear ones, but this was the *only* loss. We are to-day one people—we might have been a dozen.

During this four-years' drama I was sometimes in the audience, often behind the scenes, and once or twice upon the stage itself. When the curtain fell at last I did not appreciate the awful grandeur and moment of the events, but now I realize that they stamped their impression upon my young life. They strengthened me for undertakings for which I otherwise would have lacked nerve and endurance, and they gave me a fonder longing for the comforts of Peace than is entertained by those who have never heard the wail of woful War.

* Generals Rawlins, Porter, Badeau, Dent, and the others of General Grant's staff were at the front.

THE END.

Date Due

Demco 38-297

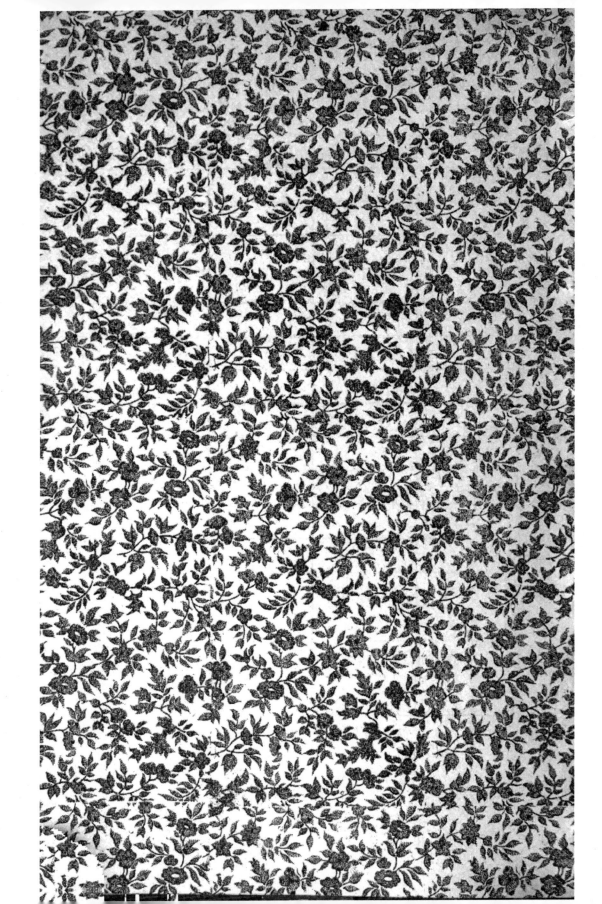

89062343439

b89062343439a

DATE DUE

MAY 21 1999	
REC'D MAR 08 1999	
MAY 21 1999	
REC'D MAY 06 1999	
STATE HISTORICAL SOCIETY	
OF WISCONSIN	
816 State Street	
Madison, Wisconsin 53706	

DEMCO, INC. 38-2931

CPSIA information can be obtained at www.ICGtesting.com
Printed in the USA
BVOW051740100112

280235BV00008B/68/P